W9-BIB-104

Great Quotes FROM Great Women

COMPILED BY
PEGGY ANDERSON

Dedication

Dedicated to my mother, Mary Crisorio,
whose unconditional love and support
have been my greatest inspiration.

...

Published by Simple Truths, LLC
1952 McDowell Road, Suite 300
Naperville, Illinois 60563

Design: Lynn Harker, Simple Truths, Illinois
Edited by: Simple Truths Editorial Team

Simple Truths is a registered trademark.
Printed and bound in the United States of America.

Photo credits : Images provided by Corbis Images and Getty Images.

800-900-3427
www.simpletruths.com

WOZ 10 9 8 7 6 5 4 3 2

Introduction

Great women are not considered so because of personal achievements, but for the effect their efforts have had on the lives of countless others. From daring feats of bravery to the understated ways of a compassionate heart, great women possess a common strength of character. Through their passion and persistence, they have advanced womanhood and the world.

These are timeless examples of individuals unafraid to challenge the status quo. These are lives and words worth remembering.

...

Peggy Anderson

Table of Contents

1744 ~ 1818

Abigail Adams

Abigail Adams was the wife of the second President of the United States of America, John Adams, and the mother of the sixth President, John Quincy Adams. To this day, she remains one of the most influential women in American history.

Like other women of her time, Abigail Adams lacked formal education; however she possessed a keen intelligence. She took a serious interest in philosophy, the classics, government and law. As First Lady, she pursued an active role in politics and policy serving as her husband John Adams' unofficial political advisor. Abigail Adams was an outspoken advocate of married women's property rights along with increased opportunities for women, particularly in the field of education. She was resolute in her disdain of slavery.

Abigail Adams was an intellectually open-minded political activist with a genuine love of her country. Her contribution as a patriot and First Lady remains invaluable.

If we do not lay out ourselves in the service of mankind, whom should we serve?

• • •

Great necessities call forth great leaders.

• • •

These are the times in which a genius would wish to live. It is not in the calm of life, or the repose of a pacific station that great characters are formed.

• • •

Learning is not attained by chance, it must be sought for with ardor and attended to with diligence.

• • •

Remember the ladies and be more generous and favorable to them than your ancestors.

• • •

We have too many high sounding words, and too few actions that correspond with them.

• • •

If we mean to have heroes, statesmen and philosophers, we should have learned women.

• • •

Arbitrary power is like most other things which are very hard, very liable to be broken.

• • •

1884 ~ 1962

Eleanor Roosevelt

Eleanor Roosevelt was a United Nations diplomat, humanitarian and wife of President Franklin D. Roosevelt.

During her twelve years as First Lady (1933-1945), the unprecedented breadth of her activities and advocacy of liberal causes made her nearly as controversial a figure as her husband. Roosevelt instituted regular White House press conferences for women correspondents for the first time. In deference to the President's illness, she helped serve as his "eyes and ears" throughout the country. She showed particular interest in such humanitarian concerns as child welfare, slum clearance projects and equal rights.

After President Roosevelt's death (1945), President Harry Truman appointed her a delegate to the United Nations, where, as chairman of the UN Commission on Human Rights, she played a major role in the drafting and adoption of the Universal Declaration of Human Rights.

Eleanor Roosevelt was one of the most widely admired women in the world and to this day continues to be an inspiration to many.

Freedom makes a huge requirement of every human being. With freedom comes responsibility. For the person who is unwilling to grow up, the person who does not want to carry his own weight, this is a frightening prospect.

• • •

Great minds discuss ideas, average minds discuss events, small minds discuss people.

• • •

Happiness is not a goal; it is a by-product.

• • •

Only a man's character is the real criterion of worth.

• • •

It isn't enough to talk about peace. One must believe in it. And it isn't enough to believe in it. One must work at it.

Justice cannot be for one side alone, but must be for both.

• • •

Life must be lived and curiosity kept alive. One must never, for whatever reason, turn his back on life.

• • •

The giving of love is an education in itself.

• • •

Understanding is a two-way street.

...

What one has to do usually can be done.

...

When you cease to make a contribution, you begin to die.

...

The future belongs to those who believe
in the beauty of their dreams.

...

Eleanor

You gain strength, courage and confidence by every experience in which you stop to look fear in the face. . . you must do the thing you think you cannot do.

• • •

It is better to light a candle than to curse the darkness.

• • •

It is not fair to ask of others what you are not willing to do yourself.

• • •

1880 ~ 1968

Helen Keller

Helen Adams Keller was born in Tuscumbia, Alabama, in 1880. A severe illness in infancy left her deprived of sight, hearing and the ability to speak. Her life represents one of the most extraordinary examples of a person who was able to transcend her physical handicaps.

Through the constant and patient instruction of Anne Sullivan, Helen Keller not only learned to read, write and speak, but went on to graduate cum laude from Radcliffe College in 1904. In addition to becoming the author of several articles, books and biographies, she was active on the staffs of the American Foundation for the Blind and the American Foundation for the Overseas Blind. She also lectured in over 25 countries and received several awards of great distinction.

Helen Keller's courage, faith and optimism in the face of such overwhelming disabilities had a profound effect on all she touched. Her tremendous accomplishments stand as a symbol of human potential.

What is very difficult at first, if we keep on trying, gradually becomes easier.

...

Alone we can do so little; together we can do so much.

...

Security is mostly a superstition. It does not exist in nature, nor do the children of men as a whole experience it. Avoiding danger is no safer in the long run than outright exposure. Life is either a daring adventure or nothing.

...

Keep your face to the sunshine and you cannot see the shadows.

...

It gives me a deep, comforting sense that 'things seen are temporal and things unseen are eternal.'

...

Happiness cannot come from without. It must come from within. It is not what we see and touch or that which others do for us which makes us happy; it is that which we think and feel and do, first for the other fellow and then for ourselves.

...

1913 ~ 2005

Rosa Parks

Growing up in Montgomery, Alabama, Rosa Parks quickly gained firsthand experience with prejudice and inequality. For years she lived with the knowledge that blacks in the South were not entitled to the same rights as those in the North.

In 1955, when Rosa Parks refused to give up her seat on a Montgomery bus to a white man, her defiance ignited a bus boycott of 381 days. Rosa Parks' action gave thousands of individuals the courage to speak out against the injustice toward Southern blacks, furthering social acceptance and equality in America.

Time magazine named Parks one of the most influential and iconic figures of the 20th century. The Rosa Parks Congressional Gold Medal bears the legend, "Mother of the Modern Day Civil Rights Movement."

Each person must live their life as a model for others.

• • •

Whatever my individual desires were to be free, I was not alone. There were many others who felt the same way.

• • •

I do the very best I can to look upon life with optimism and hope and looking forward to a better day.

• • •

Memories of our lives, of our works and our deeds will continue in others.

• • •

I have learned over the years that when one's mind is made up, this diminishes fear; knowing what must be done does away with fear.

• • •

I would like to be known as a person who is concerned about freedom and equality and justice and prosperity for all people.

• • •

I would like to be remembered as a person who wanted to be free ... so other people would be also free.

• • •

1820 ~ 1906

Susan B. Anthony

Susan B. Anthony is best remembered as a pioneer and crusader of the women's suffrage movement in the United States. President of the National American Woman Suffrage Association, her work helped pave the way for the Nineteenth Amendment to the Constitution, giving women the right to vote.

Discouraged by the limited role women were allowed in the established temperance movement, Anthony helped form the Woman's State Temperance Society in New York, one of the first organizations of its kind. She devoted herself with vigorous determination to the anti-slavery movement, serving from 1856 to the outbreak of the war in 1861, when she worked as an agent for the American Anti-Slavery Society.

Organizing the International Council of Women in 1888 and the International Woman Suffrage Alliance in 1904, Susan B. Anthony was a major catalyst for social change in America and abroad.

Men their rights and nothing more; women their rights and nothing less.

. . .

The day will come when men will recognize woman as his peer, not only at the fireside, but in councils of the nation. Then, and not until then, will there be the perfect comradeship, the ideal union between the sexes that shall result in the highest development of the race.

. . .

Susan B. Anthony

Failure is impossible.

• • •

I declare to you that woman must not depend upon the protection of man, but must be taught to protect herself, and there I take my stand.

• • •

Independence is happiness.

• • •

Cautious, careful people always casting about to preserve their reputations...can never effect a reform.

• • •

1918 ~ 2001

Mary Kay Ash

In the early 1960s, Mary Kay Ash was inspired to design a makeover of American women. Forming the cosmetics company that bears her name, she created career options for women who had never worked out of the home. Ash's objective for direct selling beauty products was to give women the opportunity to "do anything they were smart enough to do."

Mary Kay Cosmetics has grown from nine consultants and revenues of $200,000 in its first year of operation to more than 1.7 million consultants in 2008 with $2.6 billion in sales. Throughout the tremendous growth, the company founder was the recipient of numerous business honors and author of three best-selling books.

Mary Kay Ash is remembered for her executive accomplishments and contributions to female independence. She has been honored as one of the leading female entrepreneurs in the United States.

People fail forward to success.

• • •

Pretend that every single person you meet has a sign around his or her neck that says, 'Make me feel important.' Not only will you succeed in sales, you will succeed in life.

• • •

The speed of the leader is the speed of the gang.

• • •

For every failure, there's an alternative course of action. You just have to find it. When you come to a roadblock, take a detour.

• • •

A good goal is like a strenuous exercise – it makes you stretch.

• • •

Honesty is the cornerstone of all success, without which confidence and ability to perform shall cease to exist.

• • •

Ideas are a dime a dozen. People who implement them are priceless.

• • •

Don't limit yourself.
Many people limit themselves to what they think they can do.
You can go as far as your mind lets you.
What you believe, remember, you can achieve.

• • •

Most people live and die with their music still unplayed.
They never dare to try.

• • •

1954 ~

Condoleezza Rice

Not only is Condoleezza Rice the second woman to ever be named U.S. Secretary of State, she also has the noted distinction of being the first African-American woman to hold the position. Extraordinarily gifted, Rice skipped both the first and seventh grades, allowing her entrance to the University of Denver at age 15. Continuing her education, she earned two additional degrees, one being her Ph.D. in international studies.

Impressed by Rice during a 1980 fellowship, Stanford University offered her a teaching position where she remained a popular professor until her appointment to provost. In 2000, President George W. Bush appointed her National Security Advisor, resulting in the first African-American and woman in the post. Four years later, Rice again made history by being named the 66th Secretary of State.

With tenacity, intelligence and determination, Condoleezza Rice continues to shatter the glass ceilings of society.

Our work has only begun. In our time we have an historic opportunity to shape a global balance of power that favors freedom and that will therefore deepen and extend the peace. And I use the word power broadly, because even more important than military and indeed economic power is the power of ideas, the power of compassion, and the power of hope.

• • •

Foreign policy is ultimately about security—about defending our people, our society, and our values, such as freedom, tolerance, openness, and diversity.

• • •

Just because you get something doesn't mean you deserve it. And just because you deserve something doesn't mean you will get it.

• • •

*The people of the Middle East share the desire for freedom.
We have an opportunity—and an obligation—
to help them turn this desire into reality.*

• • •

Differences can be a strength.

• • •

I'm a huge proponent of exchanges, student exchanges, cultural exchanges, university exchanges. We talk a lot about public diplomacy. It's extremely important that we get our message out, but it's also the case that we should not have a monologue with other people. It has to be a conversation, and you can't do that without exchanges and openness.

• • •

1929 ~ 1994

Jacqueline Kennedy Onassis

As one of the most popular First Ladies, Jacqueline Kennedy brought elegance to the White House through her intelligence and cultured upbringing.

After becoming First Lady in 1961, Jacqueline accepted the daunting task of making the White House a home for her children, Caroline and John Jr. She then turned her attention to the rest of the White House to restore its historical essence and cultural significance. Her entertaining skills were legendary as was her social and cultural prowess, giving her a reputation for hosting magical and awe-inspiring events.

Most admire Jackie for her strength throughout the tragedy of her husband's assassination. After the death of her second husband, Aristotle Onassis, Jackie returned to New York to pursue an editing career. She continued her work until her untimely death in 1994. She remains a symbol of 20th century American fashion, poise and grace under pressure.

Jacqueline

Even though people may be well known
they still hold in their hearts the emotions of a simple person
for the moments that are the most important of those
we know on earth – birth, marriage, death.

• • •

We should all do something to right the wrongs that we see and not just complain about them.

• • •

I'll be a wife and mother first, then First Lady.

• • •

*There are many little ways
to enlarge your child's world.
Love of books is the best of all.*

• • •

One man can make a difference and every man should try.

• • •

1925 ~

Margaret Thatcher

Margaret Thatcher was the first woman in European history to be elected Prime Minister.

The daughter of a grocer, she received her degree in chemistry at Oxford, where she became president of the University Conservative Association. During the 1950s, she worked as a research chemist and also studied law, specializing in taxation.

Thatcher ran for Parliament in 1950, but it was not until 1959 that she was finally elected to the House of Commons. She served as parliamentary secretary to the Ministry of Pensions and National Insurance, and later as Secretary of State for Education and Science. She was elected the leader of the Conservative Party in 1975, and the party's victory in the 1979 elections elevated her to the office of Prime Minister.

Margaret Thatcher became known as the "Iron Lady" because of her dedication to the ideals in which she believed and the grace to get them accomplished.

What is success?
I think it is a mixture of having a flair for
the thing that you are doing;
knowing that it is not enough,
that you have got to have hard work
and a certain sense of purpose.

• • •

I am extraordinarily patient,
provided I get my own way in the end.

• • •

Europe was created by history,
America was created by philosophy.

• • •

I've got a woman's ability to stick to a job and get on with it when everyone else walks off and leaves it.

• • •

You may have to fight a battle more than once to win it.

• • •

I love argument, I love debate. I don't expect anyone to just sit there and agree with me, that's not their job.

• • •

Let our children grow tall and some taller than others if they have it in them to do so.

• • •

Margaret Thatcher

1910 ~ 1997

Mother Teresa

Mother Teresa, born Agnes Gonxha Bojaxhiu, is revered for her lifelong dedication to the poor, most notably the destitute masses of India.

In 1928, at the age of 18, she went to Ireland to join the Institute of Blessed Virgin Mary, and shortly thereafter traveled to India to work with the poor of Calcutta. After studying nursing, she moved into the slums of the city and founded the Order of the Missionaries of Charity. Mother Teresa was summoned to Rome in 1968 to found a home for the needy, and three years later, she was awarded the first Pope John XXIII Peace Prize. By the late 1970s, the Missionaries of Charity numbered more than 1,000 nuns who operated 60 centers in Calcutta and over 200 centers worldwide.

Mother Teresa's selfless commitment to helping the poor saved the lives of nearly 8,000 people in Calcutta alone. Her compassion and devotion to the destitute earned her the Nobel Peace Prize in 1979. Following her death, Mother Teresa was beatified by Pope John Paul II.

The hunger for love is more difficult to feed
than the hunger for bread.

...

We can do no great things.
We can only do small things with great love.

...

I am a little pencil in the hand of a writing God
who is sending a love letter to the world.

...

I do not pray for success. I ask for faithfulness.

...

Loneliness and the feeling of being unwanted is the most terrible poverty.

• • •

It is not how much you do, but how much love you put into the doing that matters.

• • •

Do not allow yourself to be disheartened by any failure as long as you have done your best.

• • •

To keep a lamp burning we have to put oil in it.

• • •

A joyful heart is the inevitable result of a heart burning with love.

• • •

Bring love into your home for this is where our love for each other must start.

• • •

It is not the magnitude of our actions
but the amount of love that is put into them that matters.

• • •

God doesn't require us to succeed; He only requires that we try.

• • •

Good works are links that form a chain of love.

• • •

If you can't feed a hundred people, then feed just one.

• • •

What I can do, you cannot. What you can do, I cannot.
But together we can do something beautiful for God.

• • •

Let no one ever come to you without leaving better and happier.

• • •

Mother Teresa

1867 ~ 1934

Marie Curie

Polish-born French physicist, Marie Curie, was famous for her work on radioactivity. From childhood, she was remarkable for her prodigious memory and intellect.

One of Curie's outstanding achievements was understanding the need to accumulate intense radioactive sources, not only for the treatment of illness, but also to maintain an abundant supply for research in nuclear physics. Her insights paved the way for other researchers to discover the neutron and artificial radioactivity. Shortly after this discovery, however, Marie Curie died from leukemia caused by the radiation.

Twice a winner of the Nobel Prize, Marie Curie made immense contributions to physics influencing subsequent generations of nuclear physicists and chemists.

Be less curious about people and more curious about ideas.

• • •

I was taught that the way of progress is neither swift nor easy.

• • •

*Life is not easy for any of us. But what of that?
We must have perseverance
and above all confidence in ourselves.
We must believe that we are gifted for something
and that this thing must be attained.*

• • •

Scientific work must not be considered from the point of view of the direct usefulness of it. It must be done for itself, for the beauty of science.

• • •

In science, we must be interested in things, not in persons.

• • •

After all, science is essentially international, and it is only through lack of the historical sense that national qualities have been attributed to it.

• • •

One never notices what has been done;
one can only see what remains to be done.

. . .

Nothing in life is to be feared.
It is only to be understood.

. . .

You cannot hope to build a better world without improving the individuals. To that end, each of us must work for his own improvement, and at the same time share a general responsibility for all humanity, our particular duty being to aid those to whom we think we can be most useful.

. . .

I am among those who think that science has great beauty. A scientist in his laboratory is not only a technician: he is also a child placed before natural phenomena which impress him like a fairy tale.

. . .

All of my life through, the new sights of nature made me rejoice like a child.

. . .

I am one of those who think, like Nobel, that humanity will draw more good than evil from new discoveries.

. . .

1933 ~ 2006

Ann Richards

Known for her witticism and personal charisma, Ann Richards rose through political ranks to become the first woman elected governor of Texas.

Ann's career began as a homemaker volunteering for Democratic campaigns. In her first endeavor into politics, she became Travis County commissioner, beating the incumbent in 1976. Her next post of state treasurer in 1982 brought the honor of being the first woman elected to statewide office in over 50 years.

At the pinnacle of her career, Richards became governor of Texas in 1990 where she worked to expand the power of women and minorities and to reform state prisons. In 1992, she was elected chairwoman of the Democratic National Convention. After falling prey to osteoporosis, Ann authored a novel to inspire other women to care for themselves. Even after her death, Ann is remembered as a woman of honor and integrity.

I feel very strongly that change is good because it stirs up the system.

. . .

I have very strong feelings about how you lead your life. You always look ahead, you never look back.

. . .

Teaching was the hardest work I had ever done, and it remains the hardest work I have done to date.

. . .

The here and now is all we have, and if we play it right it's all we'll need.

• • •

The public does not like you to mislead or represent yourself to be something you're not.

• • •

There is a lot more to life than just struggling to make money.

• • •

Richards

1901 ~ 1978

Margaret Mead

American anthropologist Margaret Mead's great fame owed as much to the force of her personality and outspokenness as it did to the quality of her scientific work.

As an anthropologist, she was best known for her studies of the non-literate peoples of Oceania, especially with regard to various aspects of psychology and culture, the cultural conditioning of sexual behavior, natural character and culture change. As a celebrity, she was widely known for her forays into such far-ranging topics as women's rights, childbearing, sexual morality, nuclear proliferation, race relations, drug abuse, population control, environmental pollution and world hunger.

Elected to the presidency of the American Association for the Advancement of Science at the age of 72, Margaret Mead dedicated herself to an understanding of the origins and continuing development of humanity.

Never doubt that a small group of thoughtful, committed citizens can change the world. Indeed, it is the only thing that ever has.

...

We are living beyond our means. As a people we have developed a life-style that is draining the earth of its priceless and irreplaceable resources without regard for the future of our children and people all around the world.

...

Margaret Mead

If we are to achieve a richer culture, rich in contrasting values, we must recognize the whole gamut of human potentialities, and so weave a less arbitrary social fabric, one in which each diverse human gift will find a fitting place.

...

A society which is clamoring for choice, which is filled with many articulate groups, each urging its own brand of salvation, its own variety of economic philosophy, will give each new generation no peace until all have chosen or gone under, unable to bear the conditions of choice. The stress is in our civilization.

...

1925 ~

Barbara Bush

Holding only one paying job in her life, Barbara Bush became known as an advocate of volunteerism. She met her husband George Walker Herbert Bush at a Christmas dance in 1941. After a long-distance courtship they were wed in 1945.

Barbara's priority was always her family. She supported her husband's varied careers and, in the process, managed 29 moves of the family. Once George H. took the presidency, Barbara's special cause became the promotion of a literate America. Her focus on eradicating illiteracy was the hallmark of her tenure, believing that working toward a literate America was vital to the success of the country.

In addition to literacy, she championed other causes including support for the homeless, AIDS, the elderly and school volunteer programs. She also served on the boards of directors for AmeriCares and the Mayo Clinic.

Barbara Bush's spirit of selfless humanitarianism and volunteerism has had a far-reaching impact on worthy causes throughout the United States.

If human beings are perceived as potentials rather than problems, as possessing strengths instead of weaknesses, as unlimited rather than dull and unresponsive, then they thrive and grow to their capabilities.

• • •

Some people give time, some money, some their skills and connections, some literally give their life's blood. But everyone has to give.

• • •

At the end of your life, you will never regret not having passed one more test, not winning one more verdict, or not closing one more deal. You will regret time not spent with a husband, a child, a friend, or a parent.

• • •

Giving frees us from the familiar territory of our own needs by opening our mind to the unexplained worlds occupied by the needs of others.

• • •

You just don't luck into things as much as you'd like to think you do. You build step by step, whether it's friendships or opportunities.

• • •

Never lose sight of the fact that the most important yardstick of your success will be how you treat other people – your family, friends, and coworkers, and even strangers you meet along the way.

• • •

1820 ~ 1913

Harriet Tubman

Born a slave in Maryland, Harriet Tubman yearned to be free. In 1849, she made her escape to Pennsylvania through the Underground Railroad. She then used that route 19 more times, returning to the South to lead more than 300 slaves to freedom.

As the years passed, Tubman became known as the "Moses" of her people, directing them out of an enslaved land. During the Civil War, she served the Union Army as a nurse and a spy. With black soldiers, she mobilized an effort to free slaves who had not been released by their masters.

Following the war, Tubman raised funds to construct schools for ex-slaves. She labored for female suffrage and, in 1903, established a shelter for poor, homeless blacks.

An American heroine, Harriet Tubman is remembered as an extraordinary humanitarian.

Every great dream begins with a dreamer.
Always remember you have within you
the strength, the patience, and the passion
to reach for the stars to change the world.

• • •

I freed a thousand slaves. I could have freed a thousand more
if only they knew they were slaves.

• • •

I had reasoned this out in my mind, there was one of two things
I had a right to, liberty and death. If I could not have one,
I would have the other, for no man should take me alive.

• • •

Harriet Tubman

I had crossed the line, I was free; but there was no one to welcome me to the land of freedom. I was a stranger in a strange land.

. . .

When I found I had crossed that line, I looked at my hands to see if I was the same person. There was such a glory over every thing; the sun came like gold through the trees, and over the fields, and I felt like I was in Heaven.

. . .

I grew up like a neglected weed –
ignorant of liberty, having no experience of it.

. . .

1860 ~ 1935

Jane Addams

Jane Addams was an American social reformer and pacifist, who won the Nobel Prize for Peace in 1931.

She is probably best known as the founder of Hull House, Chicago, one of the first social settlements in North America. A boarding club for working girls, Hull House offered college-level courses in various subjects and instruction in art, music and crafts. In addition to services and cultural opportunities for the largely immigrant population, Hull House trained young social workers in the practical aspects of the field.

Addams worked with labor and other reform groups for the first juvenile court law, tenement house regulations, an eight-hour working day for women, factory inspection and worker's compensation. In 1910 she became the first woman president of the National Conference of Social Work.

Jane Addams committed her life to justice for immigrants and blacks, equal rights for women and to the struggle against poverty in the United States.

Social advance depends as much upon the process through which it is secured as upon the result itself.

• • •

National events determine our ideals, as much as our ideals determine national events.

• • •

America's future will be determined by the home and the school. The child becomes largely what he is taught; hence we must watch what we teach, and how we live.

• • •

Action indeed is the sole medium of expression for ethics.

• • •

Jane Addams

Unless our conception of patriotism is progressive, it cannot hope to embody the real affection and the real interest of the nation.

• • •

Civilization is a method of living, an attitude of equal respect for all men.

• • •

In his own way each man must struggle, lest the normal law become a far-off abstraction utterly separated from his active life.

• • •

1930 ~

Sandra Day O'Connor

Sandra Day O'Connor's outstanding career has had a significant impact on the advancement of women in politics and law.

A graduate of Stanford Law School, Day was an assistant attorney general for Arizona. In 1969, this modern conservative became a Republican member of the Arizona Senate, in which she became the majority leader – the first woman in the United States to hold such a position. Her election as a Superior Court judge in Maricopa County was followed by an appointment to the Arizona Court of Appeals.

When President Ronald Reagan appointed Sandra Day O'Connor to the United States Supreme Court in 1981, she became the first female to ever sit on the High Court. She retired in 2006 to spend more time with her husband who had been diagnosed with Alzheimer's disease.

In 2008 Justice O'Connor was inducted into the Texas Women's Hall of Fame. *Forbes* magazine has listed her as one of the most powerful women in the world. Her words and wisdom continue to teach and inspire.

I don't know that there are any short cuts to doing a good job.

• • •

We pay a price when we deprive children of the exposure to the values, principles and education they need to make them good citizens.

• • •

Do the best you can in every task,
no matter how unimportant it may seem at the time.
No one learns more about a problem
than the person at the bottom.

• • •

Each of us brings to our job, whatever it is,
our lifetime of experience and our values.

...

We don't accomplish anything in this world alone ... and whatever happens is the result of the whole tapestry of one's life and all the weavings of individual threads from one to another that creates something.

...

Society as a whole benefits immeasurably from a climate in which all persons, regardless of race or gender, may have the opportunity to earn respect, responsibility, advancement and remuneration based on ability.

...

1929 ~ 1993

Audrey Hepburn

As a film and fashion icon of the 20th century, Audrey Hepburn demonstrated staunch humanitarian beliefs throughout her life.

Born in Belgium, she grew up with a passion for ballet and the stage, making her debut in the London theater. Coming to America at the age of 22, Audrey made her mark on the film industry by making 31 films and ultimately receiving five Academy Awards.

Her most notable work, however, was done off screen. Much of her time and energy was spent working with UNICEF to provide assistance to disadvantaged families in multiple Third World countries. As Goodwill Ambassador for UNICEF, Hepburn brought to the attention of the world the need for food, immunizations, and safe water in underprivileged countries. Her efforts garnered her several awards including the Presidential Medal of Freedom. Audrey Hepburn remains a legendary Hollywood humanitarian.

For beautiful eyes, look for the good in others; for beautiful lips, speak only words of kindness; and for poise, walk with the knowledge that you are never alone.

• • •

I was born with an enormous need for affection, and a terrible need to give it.

• • •

The best thing to hold onto in life is each other.

• • •

The 'Third World' is a term I don't like very much, because we're all one world.

• • •

Audrey

Living is like tearing through a museum. Not until later do you really start absorbing what you saw, thinking about it, looking it up in a book, and remembering – because you can't take it all in at once.

• • •

Taking care of children has nothing to do with politics. I think perhaps with time, instead of there being a politicization of humanitarian aid, there will be a humanization of politics.

• • •

Hepburn

1821 ~ 1912

Clara Barton

A humanitarian and founder of the American Red Cross, Clara Barton was known as the "angel of the battlefield."

At the outbreak of the Civil War, she organized an agency to obtain and distribute supplies for the relief of wounded soldiers. In 1865, at the request of President Abraham Lincoln, she set up a bureau of records to aid in the search for missing men. While Barton was in Europe for a rest, she became associated with the International Red Cross, and in 1881 she established the American Red Cross. The next year, she succeeded in having the United States sign the Geneva Agreement on the treatment of sick, wounded and dead in battle and the handling of prisoners of war.

Clara Barton is responsible for the American amendment to the constitution of the Red Cross, which provides for the distribution of relief not only in war but in times of such calamities as famines, floods, earthquakes, cyclones and pestilence.

It is wise statesmanship which suggests that in time of peace we must prepare for war, and it is no less a wise benevolence that makes preparation in the hour of peace for assuaging the ills that are sure to accompany war.

. . .

An institution or reform movement that is not selfish, must originate in the recognition of some evil that is adding to the sum of human suffering, or diminishing the sum of happiness. I suppose it is a philanthropic movement to try to reverse the process.

. . .

The door that nobody else will go in
seems always to swing open widely for me.

• • •

Economy, prudence, and a simple life are the sure masters of need,
and will often accomplish that which, their opposites,
with a fortune at hand, will fail to do.

• • •

The surest test of discipline is its absence.

• • •

I may be compelled to face danger, but never fear it.

• • •

1924 ~ 2005

Shirley Chisholm

Shirley Chisholm is the first black woman to have been elected to the United States Congress. She served the 12th Congressional District of Brooklyn for seven terms from 1968 until 1982.

Chisholm made an unprecedented bid for the presidential nomination of the Democratic Party in 1972, when she received 158 delegate votes. The campaign came one year after she helped co-found the National Women's Political Caucus (NWPC). Designed to mobilize women's political power, the NWPC encourages women to run for political office and endorses those candidates of either sex who support women's rights. She was also the founder and chairwoman of the National Political Congress of Black Women.

In 1993 Chisholm was inducted into the National Women's Hall of Fame. Through her convictions and courage, Shirley Chisholm lived true to the title of her autobiography, *Unbought and Unbossed.*

There is little place in the political scheme of things for an independent, creative personality, for a fighter. Anyone who takes that role must pay a price.

• • •

Most Americans have never seen the ignorance, degradation, hunger, sickness, and the futility in which many other Americans live . . . They won't become involved in economic or political change until something brings the seriousness of the situation home to them.

• • •

At present, our country needs women's idealism and determination, perhaps more in politics than anywhere else.

• • •

I don't measure America by its achievements but by its potential.

• • •

Service is the rent that you pay for room on this earth.

• • •

Chisholm

1830 ~ 1886

Emily Dickinson

Find ecstasy in life;
the mere sense of living is joy enough.

• • •

If I can stop one heart from breaking
I shall not live in vain.

• • •

It is better to be the hammer than the anvil.

• • •

Dickinson

1821 ~ 1910

Elizabeth Blackwell

In 1849, Elizabeth Blackwell became the first woman in the United States to become a physician. Determined to learn the intricacies of medicine, she studied privately after being refused admittance to several medical schools. Finally, Geneva Medical College in New York accepted her as a student in 1847.

As a young doctor, Blackwell raised funds to open a hospital for needy women and children. During the Civil War, she trained nurses for the Union Army and, in 1868, opened a medical school for women. In 1875, she co-founded a school of medicine for women in England and later spent her retirement years writing medical books.

A self-made and courageous woman, Elizabeth Blackwell was a pioneer in the education of women as physicians.

If society will not admit of women's free development, then society must be remodeled.

. . .

I must have something to engross my thoughts, some object in life which will fill this vacuum and prevent this sad wearing away of the heart.

. . .

It is not easy to be a pioneer – but oh, it is fascinating! I would not trade one moment, even the worst moment, for all the riches in the world.

. . .

For what is done or learned by one class of women becomes, by virtue of their common womanhood, the property of all women.

. . .

Medicine is so broad a field, so closely interwoven with general interest, dealing as it does with all ages, sexes, and classes, and yet of so personal a character in its individual applications, that it must be regarded as one of those great departments of work in which the cooperation of men and women is needed to fulfill all its requirements.

• • •

The idea of winning a doctor's degree gradually assumed the aspect of a great moral struggle, and the moral fight possessed immense attraction for me.

• • •

Elizabeth Blackwell

1940 ~ 1994

Wilma Rudolph

One of 22 children, Wilma Rudolph grew up in Tennessee. Stricken with polio at an early age, Wilma believed she would one day walk again without braces because of her mother's inspiration.

At the age of nine, the braces were removed and Rudolph spent all of her free time running and at play. In the years that followed, she was extremely active in basketball and track. She excelled as an athlete, and her years of dedication were rewarded in 1960 at the Olympic Games in Rome. Rudolph was the first woman to win three gold medals in track and field.

Wilma Rudolph passed on her skill and determination as the Track Director and Special Consultant on Minority Affairs at DePauw University. As an outstanding field and track champion, Wilma Rudolph raised women's track to the forefront in the United States.

My mother was the one who made me work,
made me believe that one day it would be possible
for me to walk without braces.

• • •

I would be very disappointed if
I were only remembered as a runner because
I feel that my contribution to
the youth of America has far exceeded
the woman who was the Olympic champion.
The challenge is still there.

• • •

Sometimes it takes years to really grasp
what has happened to your life.

• • •

Never underestimate the power of dreams and the influence of the human spirit.

• • •

No matter what accomplishments you make, somebody helps you.

• • •

The triumph can't be had without the struggle.

• • •

When the sun is shining,
I can do anything; no mountain is too high,
no trouble too difficult.

• • •

1897 ~ 1995

Margaret Chase Smith

Maine native, Margaret Chase Smith, began her political career in 1930, when at the age of 33 she became a member of the Republican State Committee.

In 1940, Smith was elected to the Seventy-Seventh Congress. Her work as an advocate for female status in the military while on the House Naval Affairs Committee earned her the title, "Mother of the Waves." The independent-thinking Congresswoman from Maine served eight years in the House of Representatives until she was elected to the U.S. Senate in 1948.

Margaret Chase Smith's honest, straightforward way gained her widespread popularity across the country and serious consideration to be America's first female vice presidential candidate.

One of the basic causes for all the trouble
in the world today is that people
talk too much and think too little.
They act impulsively without thinking.
I always try to think
before I talk.

• • •

Greatness is not manifested by unlimited pragmatism, which places such a high premium on the end justifying any means and any measures.

. . .

Moral cowardice that keeps us from speaking our minds is as dangerous to this country as irresponsible talk.

. . .

The right way is not always the popular and easy way. Standing for right when it is unpopular is a true test of moral character.

• • •

I believe that in our constant search for security we can never gain any peace of mind until we are secure in our own soul.

• • •

Margaret Chase

My creed is that public service must be more
than doing a job efficiently and honestly.
It must be a complete dedication to the people
and to the nation with full recognition that
every human being is entitled to courtesy
and consideration, that constructive criticism
is not only to be expected but sought,
that smears are not only to be expected but fought,
that honor is to be earned but not bought.

...

Smith

1928 ~

Maya Angelou

Maya Angelou overcame a troubled childhood to become a noted poet, writer and activist. Maya's first job was that of the first black female streetcar conductor. This was the first in a series of extraordinary achievements.

Early on, Angelou fine-tuned her natural dancing and acting talent to eventually earn a dance scholarship. Her performance career included a European dance tour and a plethora of television shows and records. After holding a position in the Southern Christian Leadership Conference, she moved to Egypt to edit a weekly newspaper. Two years later, Angelou became an administrator and instructor at a Ghana music school. Twice nominated for a Pulitzer Prize, Angelou also wrote an autobiographical novel series to cope with the grief she felt after Martin Luther King Jr.'s assassination on her birthday.

Through her varied experiences on life's journey, Maya Angelou is the embodiment of the American Renaissance woman.

Courage is the most important of all the virtues, because without courage you can't practice any other virtue consistently. You can practice any virtue erratically, but nothing consistently without courage.

• • •

I have found that among its other benefits, giving liberates the soul of the giver.

• • •

I've learned that making a 'living' is not the same thing as making a 'life.'

• • •

I've learned that people will forget what you said, people will forget what you did, but people will never forget how you made them feel.

• • •

I can be changed by what happens to me. But I refuse to be reduced by it.

• • •

Nothing will work unless you do.

• • •

See, you don't have to think about doing the right thing. If you are for the right thing then you do it without thinking.

• • •

The most called-upon prerequisite of a friend is an accessible ear.

. . .

I've learned that you shouldn't go through life with a catcher's mitt on both hands; you need to be able to throw something back.

. . .

We may encounter many defeats but we must not be defeated.

. . .

History, despite its wrenching pain, cannot be unlived, but, if faced with courage, need not be lived again.

. . .

The needs of a society determine its ethics.

• • •

Prejudice is a burden that confuses the past, threatens the future and renders the present inaccessible.

• • •

If we are bold, love strikes away the chains of fear from our soul.

• • •

A bird doesn't sing because it has an answer, it sings because it has a song.

• • •

1820 ~ 1910

Florence Nightingale

An English nurse, Florence Nightingale was the founder of trained nursing for women.

While in charge of nursing at a Turkish military hospital during the Crimean War (1854 – 1856), she coped with overcrowding, poor sanitation and a shortage of basic medical supplies. As Nightingale made her nightly hospital rounds she gave comfort and advice, establishing the image of "The Lady with the Lamp" among the wounded.

Regarded as an expert on public hospitals, she was dedicated to improving the health and living conditions of the British soldier. In 1860, she founded the Nightingale School for Nurses, the first such school of its kind in the world.

Florence Nightingale has been immortalized as the epitome of tender care.

I attribute my success to this –
I never gave or took any excuse.

• • •

I never lose an opportunity of urging a practical beginning, however small, for it is wonderful how often the mustard-seed germinates and roots itself.

• • •

I can stand out the war with any man.

• • •

Florence

I stand at the altar of the murdered men,
and, while I live, I fight their cause.

• • •

How very little can be done
under the spirit of fear.

• • •

Were there none who were discontented with what they have,
the world would never reach anything better.

• • •

Nightingale

1905 ~ 1992

Clara McBride Hale

A devoted and loving mother, Clara McBride Hale raised her own children, along with over 30 other youngsters. Her unconditional love for children led this remarkable woman to open Hale House in Harlem, New York, during the early 1970s.

Hale House was a desperately needed center for infants born to drug-addicted mothers. In the midst of poverty, this program provided nurturing, love and medical attention to those helpless babies of families who also received care and rehabilitation. The legacy and love of this extraordinary woman lives on within the walls of the Hale House.

In 1985, "Mother" Clara McBride Hale was named an "American Hero" by President Ronald Reagan. The Living Legacy Award was dedicated to the memory of the giving and selfless Clara Hale in 1993.

If you can't hold children in your arms,
please hold them in your hearts.

• • •

Being black does not stop you.
You can sit out in the world and say,
'Well, white people kept me back, and I can't do this.' Not so.
You can have anything you want if you make up your mind
and you want it.

• • •

Clara Mc

Until I die, I'm going to keep doing. My people need me. They need somebody that's not taking from them and is giving them something.

• • •

When I'm gone, somebody else will take it up and do it. This is how we've lived all these years.

• • •

I'm not an American hero. I'm a person who loves children.

• • •

1897 ~ 1937

Amelia Earhart

An American aviator, Amelia Earhart was the first woman to fly solo across the Atlantic Ocean.

After a Kansas upbringing and education, she learned to fly in California, taking up aviation as a hobby. Following a series of record flights, she made a solo trans-Atlantic flight from Harbour Grace, Newfoundland, to Ireland and later flew the first solo from Hawaii to the American mainland.

In June 1937, Earhart attempted the first round-the-world flight near the equator. After taking off on July 1 from New Guinea for Howland Island in the Pacific, her plane vanished. A great naval search failed to locate her and it was assumed that she had been lost at sea.

The mystery and fascination surrounding Amelia Earhart's life and death continue to this day. The most current research confirmed the discovery of portions of her aircraft on a small, remote island in the Pacific.

No kind action ever stops with itself.
One kind action leads to another.
Good example is followed.

• • •

A single act of kindness throws out roots in all directions, and the roots spring up and make new trees.

• • •

Better do a good deed near at home
than go far away to burn incense.

• • •

Amelia

Adventure is worthwhile in itself.

• • •

*Never interrupt someone
doing what you said couldn't be done.
You can do anything you decide to do.
You can act to change and control your life,
the process is its own reward. Women,
like men, should try to do the impossible.
And if they fail, their failure
should be a challenge to others.*

• • •

Earhart

1898 ~ 1978

Golda Meir

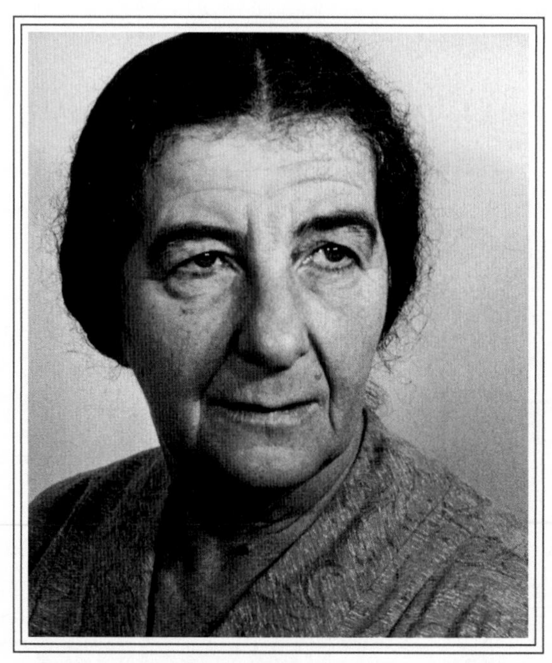

Golda Meir was a founder of the State of Israel, and served as its fourth Prime Minister. Born in Kiev, Ukraine, she emigrated to Wisconsin in 1906. Her political activity began as a leader in the Milwaukee Labor Zionist Party.

After emigrating to Palestine in 1921, she held key posts in the Jewish Agency and in the World Zionist Organization. After Israel proclaimed its independence in 1948, she served as minister of labor, and then foreign minister. Meir was appointed Prime Minister in 1969.

During her administration, she worked for a peace settlement in the Middle East using diplomatic means. Her efforts at forging peace were halted by the outbreak of the fourth Arab-Israeli war. She resigned her post in 1974, but remained an important political figure throughout her retirement.

Golda Meir's true strength and spirit were emphasized when after her death in 1978, it was revealed that she had suffered from leukemia for 12 years.

Golda Meir

*I never did anything alone.
Whatever was accomplished in this country
was accomplished collectively.*

• • •

I must govern the clock, not be governed by it.

• • •

*I have faced difficult problems in the past
but nothing like the one I'm faced with
now in leading the country.*

• • •

Don't be humble.
You aren't that great.

• • •

Old age is like a plane flying through a storm.
Once you're aboard, there's nothing you can do.

• • •

One cannot and must not try to erase the past
merely because it does not fit the present.

• • •

You'll never find a better sparring partner than adversity.

• • •

Trust yourself.
Create the kind of self that you will be
happy to live with all of your life.
Make the most of yourself by fanning the tiny,
inner sparks of possibility
into flames of achievement.

• • •

Golda

Those who do not know how to weep with their whole heart don't know how to laugh either.

• • •

I can honestly say that I was never affected by the question of the success of an undertaking. If I felt it was the right thing to do, I was for it regardless of the possible outcome.

• • •

Meir

About the Author

OVER THE PAST twenty years, Peggy Anderson has compiled more than a dozen quotation books on various topics. Her books have sold more then 500,000 copies.

• • •